All About...

Rabbits and Other Small Animals

Fun facts and tips about your pets

Contents

Each year, thousands of unwanted rabbits and rodents are rehomed by the RSPCA.

This book has been created to help you to give your pet rabbits or rodents a happy, healthy life. Read on and find out all about them.

Quick quiz: rabbits

So you think you know all about rabbits and other small animals? Take this true or false quiz to see how much you really know:

1 The main food rabbits eat is carrots.

2 Rabbits are best kept with guinea pigs.

3 Rabbits are most active during the day.

4 Rabbits are best kept on their own.

5 Rabbits eat their droppings when they are bored.

Answers

1. False! Turn to page 77 to find out more about what pet rabbits should eat.

2. False! Turn to page 64 for more about suitable pairings for rabbits.

3. False! Turn to page 14 and 66 for more about rabbit behaviour.

4. False! Rabbits are social animals and prefer to live in groups.

5. False! Turn to page 76 to find out why rabbits and some other animals eat their droppings.

Meet the rabbit family

Rabbits are small, furry mammals with large ears, long back legs, big front teeth and short tails. Their bodies are built for getting away from hungry predators who munch on cute little bunnies for lunch. Rabbits aren't rodents, like rats and mice. Instead, they belong to a small group of animals called lagomorphs, which means 'hare-like'. Other lagomorphs include pikas and hares.

Did you know?

A male rabbit is called a buck.

A female rabbit is called a doe.

A baby rabbit is called a kitten.

Wild rabbit relations

Wild rabbits found in Britain live in big, family groups in burrows they dig in the ground. They spend about three-quarters of their time above ground, grazing on grass and other plants. But, at the first sign of danger, they turn tail and bolt for cover.

European brown hares are bigger than rabbits with longer ears and longer legs. Unlike European rabbits, they're normally loners and live in simple hollows in the ground called 'forms'. Luckily, they're super-speedy runners and can hare away from danger at speeds of over 70 kilometres per hour.

Pikas have round ears and short legs. They are found in mountains, forests and meadows. In summer, they collect little piles of leaves, grass and seeds to live on in the winter. Some pikas pop stones on top to stop the piles blowing away in the wind.

Did you know?

For thousands of years, people hunted wild rabbits for their meat and fur. The first rabbits to reach Britain may have been brought by Roman soldiers, to be killed for the pot.

Top five wild rabbit facts

5 An Alaskan hare's enormous! It weighs as much as four normal-sized bunnies!

4 The black-tailed jackrabbit's whopping ears aren't just useful for listening out for predators. They also lose heat, keeping the jackrabbit cool as a cucumber in its desert home.

3 Snowshoe hares get their name from their huge back feet. These work like snowshoes and stop it sinking into the deep snow where it lives. Its feet are also hairy to keep them warm and help them to grip.

2 The Arctic hare has a cunning way of staying hidden from enemies. In winter, it grows a white coat to match the snow. In summer, it grows a brown-grey coat to match the ground.

1 The titchy volcano rabbit wins the prize for the most explosive home. It lives in patches of pine forest that grow on the slopes of four extinct volcanoes in Mexico.

Body design

Rabbits' bodies have lots of features to help them get away from danger, and stay alive.

Long, mobile ears for sharp hearing

Big, beady eyes for spotting predators and seeing well at dawn and dusk, when they are most active

Long whiskers for sensing

Long front teeth for biting plants

Large feet and claws for running and digging

Long, strong back legs for hopping and thumping

Did you know?

While they're grazing, rabbits keep standing up on their back feet to look around. If they spot danger, they thump their feet on the ground to warn the others. When they run, their white tail flashes up and down, signalling to other rabbits that they need to run, too.

Soft fur for warmth and camouflage

Soft, fluffy tail with white underside – used to signal danger to other rabbits

Did you know?

If rabbits are chased, they run off quickly but not in a straight line. They scamper and dash about to try to confuse their attackers.

Rabbit senses

In the wild, rabbits need to stay alert at all times, especially when they're grazing above ground. Luckily, they've got super-sharp senses...

• **Sight:** rabbits have big, round eyes set on the sides of their heads, which means that rabbits can see almost all the way around them, but not quite. The position of their eyes means they have a blind spot just in front of their nose, so they can't see what they are eating up close!

• **Hearing:** having big ears is brilliant for hearing. A rabbit can prick up its ears and move them about to hear even soft, far-away sounds.

• **Smell:** ever seen a rabbit twitching its nose? It's keeping a nose out for danger. Rabbits have a very strong sense of smell for sniffing out other rabbits, and danger.

• **Touch:** a rabbit's whiskers are stiff hairs around its mouth, nose, cheeks and eyes. The whiskers are as long as the rabbit's body is wide. This makes them useful for judging holes and other spaces to see if there's enough room for the rabbit to squeeze inside.

Did you know?

Rabbits also use smells to mark out their territory. They do this by weeing, leaving droppings and by rubbing smells from their chins onto objects, which makes them smell familiar and reassuring to them.

Rabbit tales

Over the centuries, many rabbits have burrowed their way into people's stories and beliefs. Here are some things you might not know about rabbits, but which do you believe?

In some countries, it's good luck to say, 'Rabbit, rabbit, rabbit', or, 'White rabbits', out loud on the first day of the month.

An ancient tradition says that carrying a rabbit's foot is lucky (though not for the rabbit). Some people carry a front foot; some people a back foot. Other people say that the rabbit must have been killed with a silver bullet or at the time of a new moon.

In the Chinese zodiac, each year is linked to an animal. People born in the Year of the Rabbit are said to be kind and gentle, with a sense of fun. They get on well with others, are good with money and don't like being away from home.

Aztec legend says that a rabbit lives on the moon – you can see its shape when there is a full moon. The gods threw the rabbit at the moon to stop it shining as brightly as the sun.

In Native American stories, Rabbit is a cunning character who gets his way by playing tricks. In one story, he escapes from being eaten by wolves by teaching them how to dance. While they are dancing, he hops away to safety across a field.

Famous bunnies of books and films

Rabbits have also had leading roles in many books, films and cartoons. In between takes in their busy schedules, we caught up with four of these floppy-eared stars...

4 Peter Rabbit

Peter Rabbit stars in books by Beatrix Potter. In one story, he disobeys his mother and sneaks into Mr McGregor's garden where he munches on some prized veg. Mr McGregor chases him off with his gun, and Peter has a very lucky escape.

3 Hazel

Watership Down is a novel by Richard Adams. It stars a group of rabbits who have to find a new home when their warren is destroyed. The main character is a rabbit called Hazel. He is brave, loyal and wise, and leads the rabbits on their dangerous journey.

2 Bugs Bunny

Bugs Bunny is a grey cartoon rabbit who's usually seen chewing on a carrot. He is famous for his catchphrase, 'What's up, doc?' and for getting himself out of trouble by outsmarting anyone who crosses him.

1 Harvey

In the film *Harvey*, a man called Elwood P. Dowd makes friends with an imp-like creature which takes the shape of a two-metre-tall, invisible rabbit – Harvey. By the end of the film, Elwood's friends, family, and even his doctor, have come to believe in Harvey, too.

Rabbits to the rescue

It's not only in well-loved books and Hollywood films that rabbits are heroes. Here are the true-life tales of two amazingly brave bunnies who saved their owners' lives...

FACT FILE

Remarkable rabbit

Dory, a rabbit from Cambridgeshire, in England, performed a remarkable feat in 2004.

When her owner, Simon Steggall, seemed to fall asleep, his wife thought nothing about it. It was only when Dory starting thumping on his chest that she realized something was badly wrong and called for an ambulance. In fact, Simon had diabetes and had fallen into a coma. Without devoted Dory, he'd probably have died.

FACT FILE

A sad tail

In 2011, a woman living in Alaska, USA, was woken up early in the morning by her pet rabbit scratching on her chest. Immediately, she smelled smoke and realized that her house was on fire. Thanks to her pet's quick thinking, she and her daughter were able to escape the fire unharmed.

Top five pet rabbit facts

5 Rabbits were first kept as pets about 400 years ago. Pet rabbits are descended from wild European rabbits.

4 In the UK, there are thought to be over 1.7 million pet rabbits. Excluding fish, this makes rabbits the third most popular pet after cats and dogs.

3 Rabbits are most active in the early morning and late evening. Sometimes they are active overnight, too.

2 Pet rabbits usually live for around 8-12 years but the oldest on record reached the incredible age of 16!

1 Rabbits are intelligent animals. They can be trained using healthy treats and gentle encouragement to come to you when they are called!

Did you know?

Here are some of the top pet rabbit names:

• Thumper • Fluffy • Snowy • Flopsy • Bunny • Floppy • Fudge • Bugsy • Daisy

All kinds of rabbits

There are lots of different kinds, or breeds, of pet rabbits. They come in all sorts of sizes, shapes and coat types. Although many people like certain breeds of rabbit because they have a particular appearance, they can suffer from health problems if they have exaggerated features such as extra-long ears. Rabbits that are a mixture, or 'cross-breed', tend to be healthier and are just as beautiful!

Rabbits vary in size, from small rabbits that weigh around 0.9 kg when fully grown, all the way up to giant breeds which can weigh more than a domestic cat. Take time to pick pets that are right for you and your home. Larger rabbits will need more space, while long-haired rabbits will need gentle daily grooming, so it is always wise to think about these things before you commit to getting your pets.

It's best not to choose a pet because their particular breed is meant to be 'friendly' or looks 'cute'. Just like people, rabbits all have different personalities. Sadly, there are always lots of rabbits in rescue centres who need re-homing. The staff will be able to advise you on which ones may be suitable for your home and family.

Quick quiz: rodents

So you think you know about rodents? Test your knowledge with this quick quiz.

1. Hamsters are nocturnal.
2. Rodents live on every continent.
3. The rat is the first sign in the Chinese zodiac.
4. Rats can be trained.
5. Mice should be kept away from things like TVs and running water.

6 Some rodents, such as chinchillas need dirt baths to stay clean.

7 A prehistoric species of giant rat weighed the same as a car.

8 Syrian and golden hamsters are best suited to living in groups.

Answers

1. True – for more on hamster behaviour, turn to page 45.

2. False – they don't live in Antarctica.

3. True – turn to page 36 to find out more.

4. True – to find out more about their extraordinary work, turn to page 40.

5. True – turn to page 75 to find out more about homes for mice.

6. True – for more about chinchillas, turn to page 81.

7. True. Turn to page 37 to find out more.

8. False – for information on hamster groups turn to page 65.

Meet the rodent family

Squirrels, dormice, capybaras, beavers, porcupines and chinchillas... What do they have in common? They're all rodents, that's what.

In fact, rodents make up more than 40 per cent of all mammal species. That's an awful lot of rodents and they get everywhere. They live in every habitat, on every continent, apart from Antarctica.

Did you know?

Can't tell your rodents and rabbits apart? Rodents have only one pair of upper incisors – sharp teeth used for gnawing. Rabbits, which belong to the lagomorph family, have two pairs of upper front teeth, one behind the other.

Rodent relations

Ready to meet a selection of other rodent relations? Here's a quick spotter's guide...

Beaver

Dormouse

Squirrel

Capybara
Porcupine
Chinchilla
Spiny rat

Top six wild rodent facts

6 Capybaras from South America are the biggest rodents around today. They look quite like guinea pigs, except that they're about the size of sheep!

5 The record for the laziest rodent goes to the... Arctic ground squirrel. This sleepyhead hibernates for five to seven months of the year in its cosy underground burrow.

4 Mole rats are brilliant burrowers. Using its chisel-like incisor teeth for digging, it can shift as much as 50 times its own weight in soil in just 20 minutes.

3 Flying squirrels can't actually fly but they can glide from tree to tree. Their front and back legs are joined by furry folds of skin that work like a parachute.

2 When it's threatened, a North American porcupine sticks out its 30,000 quills so that it looks like a giant pincushion. Usually that is enough to scare off a would-be attacker!

1 The master builders of the rodent world are beavers. They build huge dams across rivers and streams, using their super-strong teeth to chop down trees.

Top five rodents of myth and history

Rodents often pop up in people's stories and beliefs, though not all of these stories have happy endings...

5 In Hindu myth, the elephant-headed god, Ganesh, often has a rat or mouse at his feet. Legend says that he tamed the rat so that he could ride on it.

4 The rat is the first of the twelve signs of the Chinese zodiac. A person born in the year of the Rat is believed to be quick-thinking, active and charming.

3 Viking myths tell of Ratatosk, a squirrel, that runs up and down the trunk of Yggdrassil, the world tree. It carries insults between an evil dragon that lives among the tree's roots, and an eagle that lives on its highest branches.

2 Some prehistoric rodents grew to a massive size. A giant rat discovered in South America in 2007 lived around 2-4 million years ago. It weighed as much as a car!

1 Between 1347 and 1351, black rats were responsible for wiping out a quarter of the population of Europe – about 25 million people. They carried fleas that passed on the Black Death, or plague.

Did you know?

Sailors used to think that rats deserting a ship before it set sail meant that it would sink on its voyage. If they ran away from a building, it was a sign that it would soon be on fire.

Rodents in books and films

Have you heard the nursery rhyme about the three blind mice? Rodents play starring parts in many books, films, poems, cartoons and fairy tales...

Wind in the Willows

The Wind in the Willows is a children's book by Kenneth Grahame. It tells the story of four animals – Mole, Badger, Ratty (a water rat) and Toad – whose quiet, riverside life is turned upside-down when Toad gets a car.

Mickey Mouse

One of the world's most famous cartoon characters, Mickey Mouse, wears white gloves, red shorts, and big yellow shoes. He was created in 1928 by Walt Disney who based him on his own pet mouse. Mickey has a girlfriend, Minnie Mouse, and a pet dog, Pluto.

Pied Piper of Hamelin

In this German fairy tale, the Pied Piper gets rid of the rats from the town of Hamelin. The rats follow the sound of his magic pipe to the river, where they drown. But when the piper isn't paid, he turns his magic on the town's children, leading them away, never to return.

Ratatouille

Ratatouille is a film set in France and stars Remy, a rat who dreams of becoming a famous chef. He makes friends with a boy who works in a restaurant, and starts cooking in secret, afraid that the customers wouldn't like the food if they knew who'd really made it. His best dish is ratatouille, a tasty vegetable stew.

Rescue rodents

It’s not only rabbits that come to the rescue. Believe it or not, rats can be life-savers, too.

FACT FILE

Time to head to Africa to meet the HeroRATS...

In Africa, giant pouched rats are being trained to find landmines buried under the ground. These mines were left behind in wars. They kill thousands of people each year when they accidentally step on them. With their superb sense of smell, the rats are brilliant at sniffing the mines out. Then the mines can be safely destroyed.

The rats work for peanuts. It's true! They learn to recognize a landmine smell in return for peanuts or bananas. Training takes about nine months, then the rats are ready for the real deal. They wear special harnesses, attached to leads. When they find a landmine, they warn their handlers by scratching on the ground.

The HeroRATS are so good at their job, it's hoped to train them to find survivors buried after earthquakes, and to detect the deadly disease of tuberculosis, or TB.

Strange but true

Pet fit for a president

Theodore Roosevelt was President of the USA from 1933-1945. The animal-mad president had loads of pets, including several dogs, cats, a one-legged chicken, a snake, called Emily Spinach, a badger, several guinea pigs and a rat, called Jonathan.

Did you know?

Jack Black was royal rat-catcher to Queen Victoria. He kept some of the rats with unusual fur colouring and it is said he was the first person to keep rats as pets.

Pet rodents: a spotter's guide

To help you choose the right rodents for your family, here's a quick guide to the most popular pet rodents...

Guinea pigs

Guinea pigs are small and stocky with short legs and no tail. They come in many different colours and can have short or long hair. Long-haired breeds require grooming every day, which is a big commitment, so for new owners, short-haired varieties may be a better choice. Guinea pigs are sociable and chatty, making lots of squeaking, grunting, chirping and even purring sounds.

Gerbils

With their long back legs, gerbils' bodies are built for digging burrows to hide from predators in their wild, desert home. Gerbils can be quite timid creatures and need to be handled very gently and regularly from a young age so they learn to see people as friends.

Hamsters

Hamsters are small with tiny tails. They are nocturnal which means that they are active at night and need peace and quiet during the day. Bulging cheeks are another hamster feature – it's how they carry food to their larder.

Mice

Mice are the smallest pet rodents of those mentioned in this book, with small ears and long tails. They're most active at dawn, dusk and during the night, when they enjoy playing, building nests and foraging for food. They need peace and quiet during the day.

Rats

Rats look very similar to mice but they are bigger, have scalier tails and they can be more active during the day. With the right care they can make rewarding pets. They're curious and clever, with good memories and can easily be trained. They will get bored if they don't have plenty to do.

Chinchillas

Chinchillas have large ears, strong back legs, tails that take up a third of their bodies and masses of soft, silky fur. They're brilliant at jumping and need loads of space for exercise. They're shy and like quiet during the day when they are sleeping and resting. Teens and adults are most able to meet their needs.

Did you know?

Degus look a bit like gerbils but are bigger and have long, silky coats, with long, tufty tails. In the wild, they come from the Andes mountains in South America where they live in small family groups.

The top five small, but perfectly formed pet rodent facts

5 Guinea pigs aren't pigs and they don't come from Guinea, a country in Africa. So where does their name come from? In the 17th century, when guinea pigs first came to Europe, the word 'guinea' meant 'strange'. But no one really knows for certain.

4 Since ancient times, people in South America have eaten guinea pig meat and offered guinea pig sacrifices to the gods. Today, guinea pigs are still eaten– roasted, fried, barbequed and in guinea pig soup. Don't let your pet guinea pigs hear that!

3 Golden hamsters are also called Syrian hamsters and they like to live on their own, while types of dwarf hamster usually like to have company of other friendly hamsters of their own type, or 'species'.

2 Gerbils come from the desert. They have special features to help them survive, such as being able to get water from the food they eat. To stop water being wasted, gerbils also do very dry poos and only do a couple of drops of wee at a time.

1 Chinchillas have thick fur to keep them warm in their wild, mountain homes. Each of their skin's hair follicles grows 60-90 hairs, compared to only one on you!

Rodent senses

Rodents have super-sharp senses to find their way, sniff out food and keep out of danger.

Why not get a rodent's-eye view of the world with this quick quiz? Do you think...

1. Hamsters have super-sharp eyesight? True/False

2. Hamster use their whiskers to explore? True/False

3. Rats like wide, open spaces? True/False

4 Chinchillas 'freeze' if they're scared? True/False

5 Mice can't smell a thing?
True/False

Answers

1 False. Hamsters have big, beady eyes for seeing in the dark. But they're very short-sighted and can only see a few centimetres in front of their noses.

2 True. Hamsters and other rodents twitch their whiskers to feel around.

3 False. Rats hate wide open spaces because there's nowhere for them to hide. If you have pet rats, be sure to give them at least one safe hiding place each.

4 True. If a chinchilla's frightened, it stays completely still or will dash for cover. Chinchillas have very sharp hearing and are easily spooked by loud noises so they need a nice, quiet home.

5 False. Mice and rats have an amazing sense of smell. They can sniff out friends and enemies, food and other animals' territories (mice mark these out with smelly wee).

Are you a top pet owner?

With the right care and in the right hands, rabbits and rodents can make rewarding pets but would you make a brilliant pet owner?

Here are some of the questions to ask yourself if you are thinking of getting small pets.

7 Can you give them a good home, with lots of space, suitable bedding and time to rest undisturbed when they need to sleep?

6 Can you give them the right amount of healthy food and fresh, clean water every day?

5 Can you take them to the vet's if they're ill and afford the vet's bill?

4 Can you make sure they have suitable toys, places to hide and things to do?

Did you know?

Owning pet rabbits or rodents is a big responsibility. If you own or look after pets, you must care for them properly and meet all their needs to make sure they are happy and healthy – that's the law.

3. Can you make sure your pet has suitable company, either with another friendly animal of the same species/type, or gentle companionship with you if they need to be kept on their own?

2. Can you make sure they are looked after if you're away?

1. Can you care for them for the rest of their life?

Answers

To be a top pet owner, you need to answer YES to every question and many more besides. You also need to make sure your parents/guardian agrees to you having pets and will help you care for them. If you answered NO to any questions, think again about getting pets.

Choosing your rabbit

If you are positive you can give pet rabbits a happy and healthy home and care for them properly, you are ready to think about what type of rabbit is right for you and your family.

It's easy to fall head-over-heels in love with the first fluffy bunnies you see, but you should also check that they are happy and healthy. Here are some things to look out for.

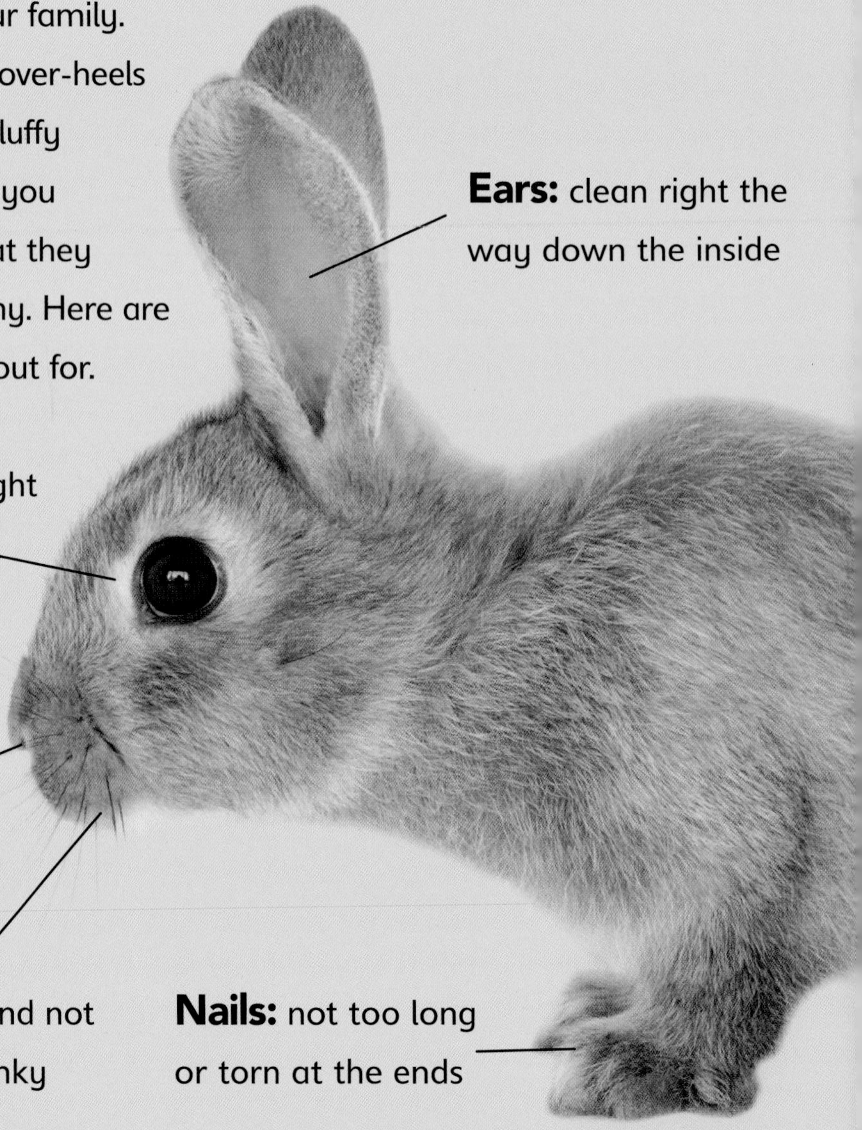

Ears: clean right the way down the inside

Eyes: clear and bright with no watery or crusty discharge

Nose: clean and twitching, with no runniness or sneezing

Teeth: clean and not too long or wonky

Nails: not too long or torn at the ends

Did you know?

Animal rescue centres are always looking for good homes for friendly pairs or groups of rabbits. New owners should ensure their pets are neutered, vaccinated and microchipped.

Coat: clean and glossy, well groomed with no fur loss

Weight: correct weight and with good body condition; not too fat or thin

Tail and bottom: clean, with no matted fur or signs of diarrhoea/droppings that are stuck or wee stains

Feet: no signs of soreness (redness, fur loss) on the bottom of their feet

Choosing your pet rodent

If it's pet rodents you're looking for, you need to choose a type that you can look after properly. On these two pages you can find out what to look for when your are choosing your new pets.

Guinea pigs

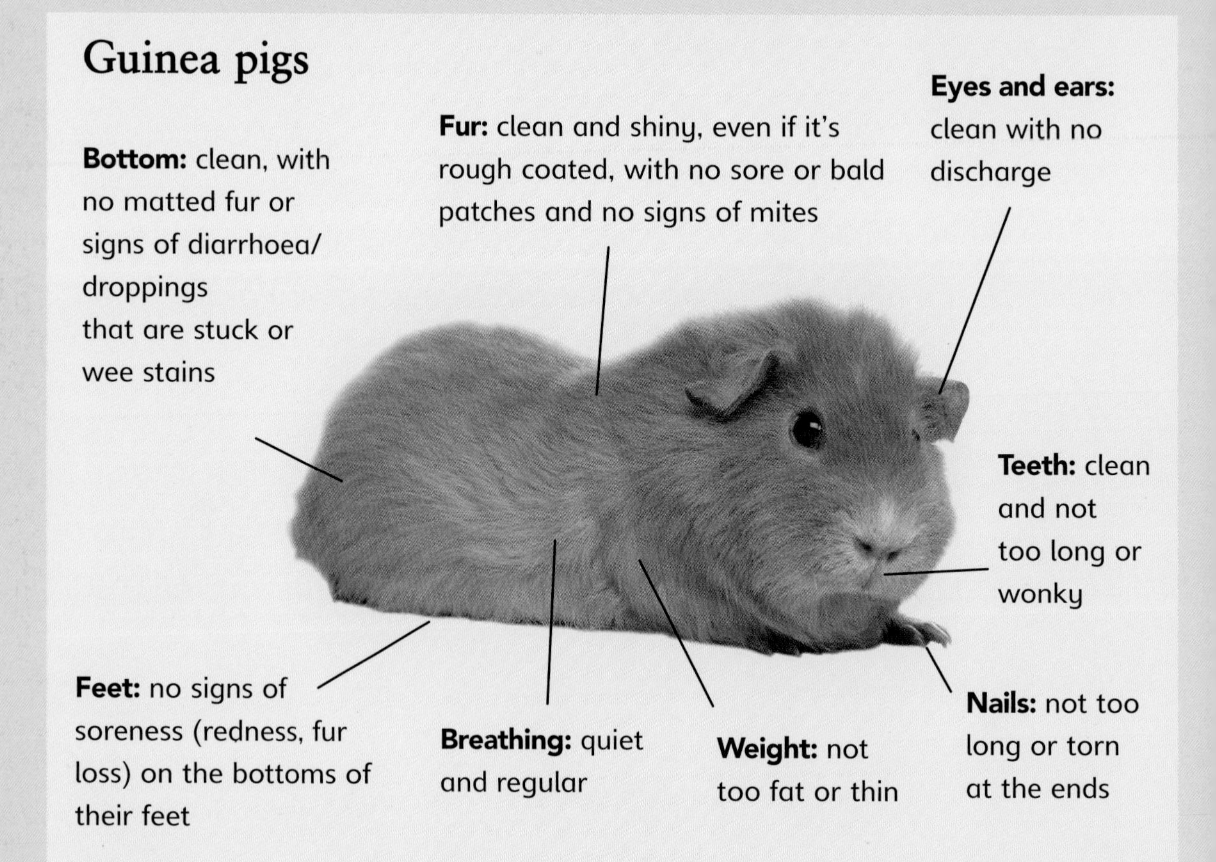

Top tip: It's best to choose short-haired guinea pigs for your first pets. Rough-coated and long-haired guinea pigs need grooming every day.

Hamsters

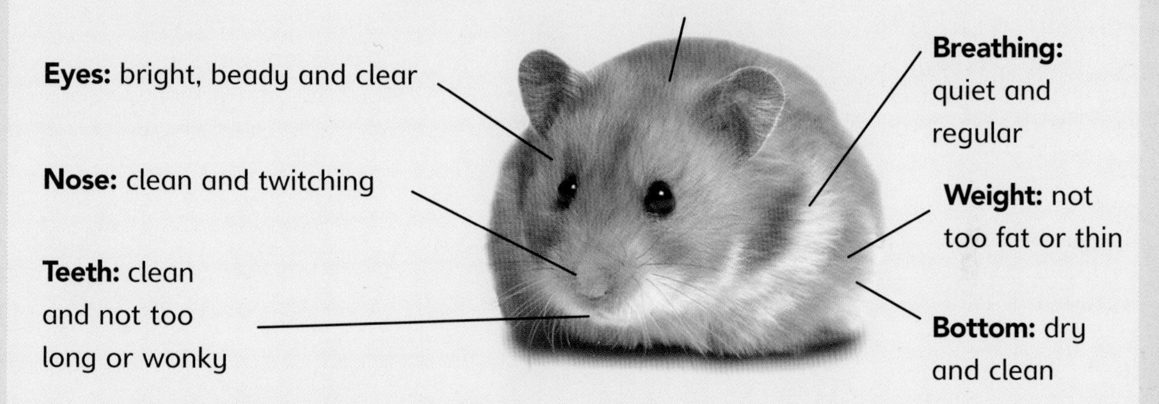

Top tip: Never disturb your hamster if it is sleeping – it may get scared and bite you.

Gerbils

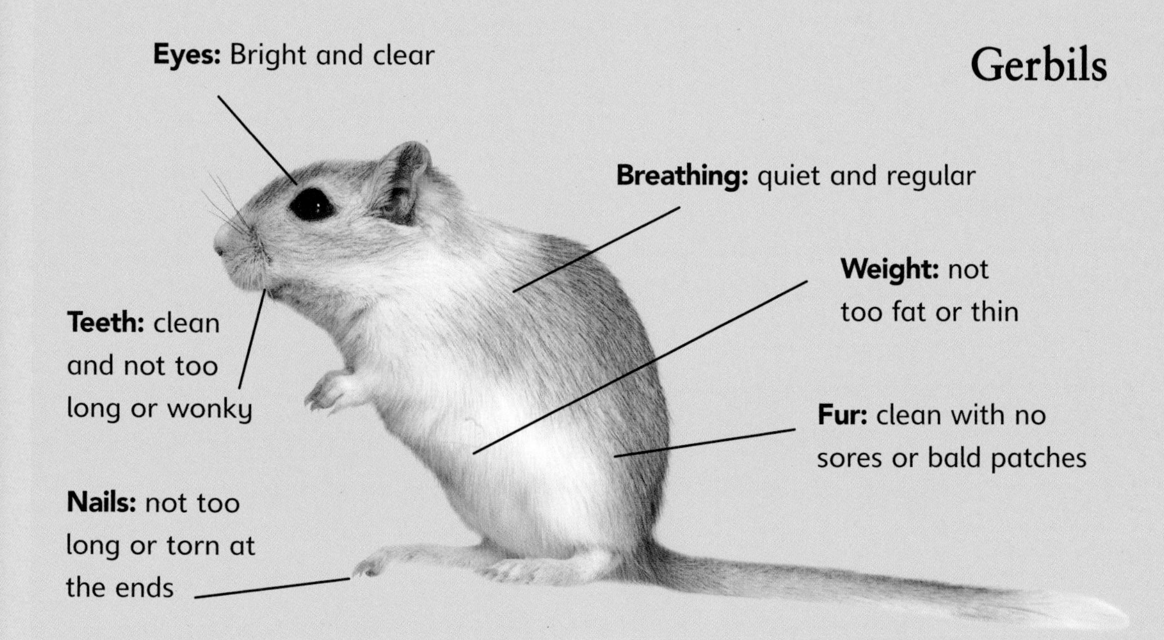

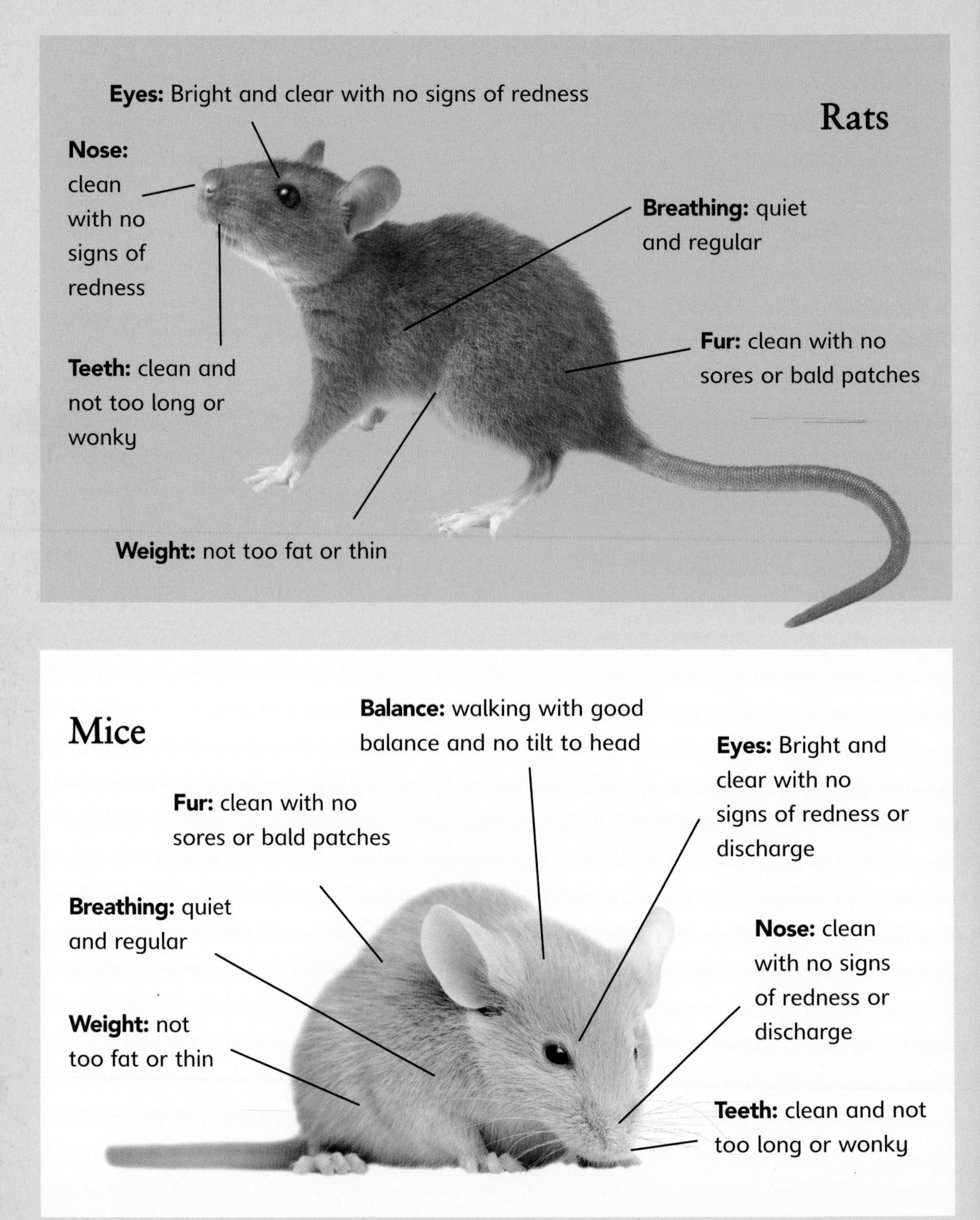
Rats
Eyes: Bright and clear with no signs of redness
Nose: clean with no signs of redness
Breathing: quiet and regular
Fur: clean with no sores or bald patches
Teeth: clean and not too long or wonky
Weight: not too fat or thin
Mice
Balance: walking with good balance and no tilt to head
Eyes: Bright and clear with no signs of redness or discharge
Fur: clean with no sores or bald patches
Breathing: quiet and regular
Nose: clean with no signs of redness or discharge
Weight: not too fat or thin
Teeth: clean and not too long or wonky

Chinchillas

Chinchillas are shy animals, who are more suited as pets for older children and adults.

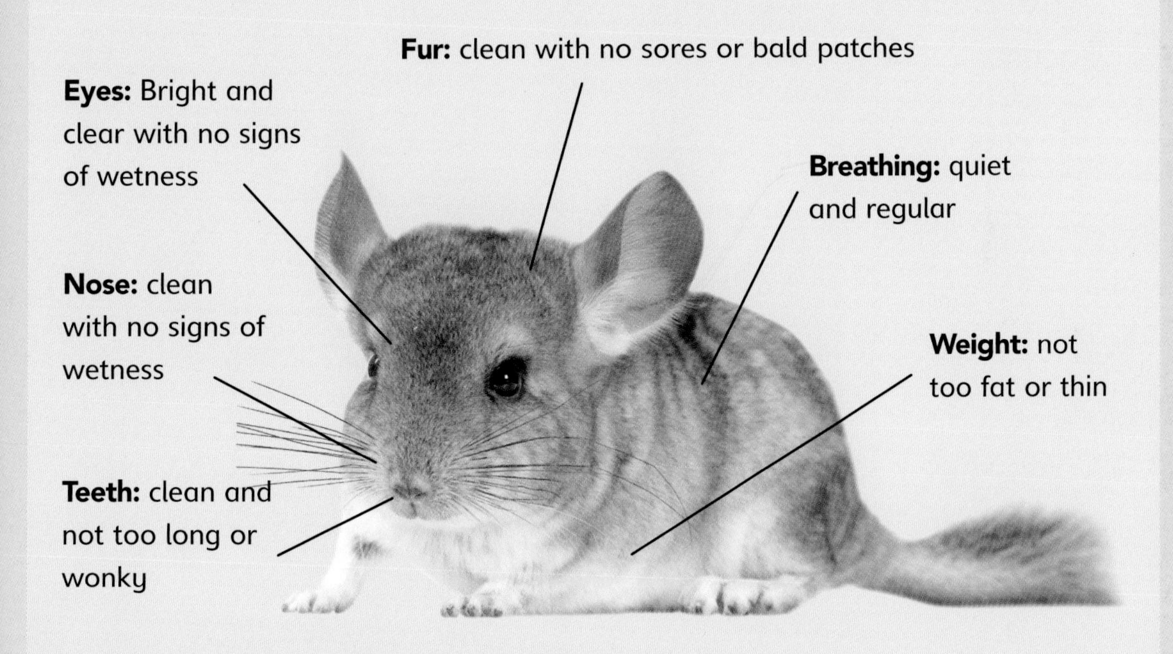

Did you know?

Animal rescue centres are always looking for good, caring homes for their rabbits and rodents whose previous owner may not be able to look after them anymore.

Coming home

You've picked out your new pets and it's time to bring them home. This is exciting for you but can be scary for your rabbits or rodents. Follow these top tips for transporting your pets and helping them to settle in.

The top five home-coming tips

5 Bring your pets home in a sturdy pet carrier – cardboard carriers are not great because they can get wet and your pets can chew through them! Make sure that it's shut properly. Put some soft bedding and nesting material inside that already smells of your pets to make them comfortable.

4 Cover the carrier with something like a towel to keep it dark but make sure that plenty of air can still flow so that your pets can breathe easily. Make sure that your pets don't get too hot or too cold.

3 When you get home, put your pets in their new enclosure or cage and make sure that they have everything they need. Leave them to rest undisturbed for a few hours, so they can start getting used to their new home.

2 Make sure that each of your pets has a place where they can hide if they feel scared. Rabbits and rodents are prey species and so have to hide from predators in the wild; pet rodents need to be able to hide whenever they feel afraid or need some time away from their companions or people.

1 Never leave your pets alone with other pets, such as cats and dogs or people that may deliberately or accidentally hurt or frighten them.

Did you know?

Before you bring your pets home, get everything ready. Over the next few pages, you can find out which bits of kit you'll need.

Handle with care

It's good to get your pet used to being handled from an early age – check with a vet as to the best age to start from and how to do this for your pet. It's always best to let an adult pick up your pet and to show you how to handle them safely.

Make sure you have a grown-up with you to help you when you are looking after your pet and remember to be extremely careful with them. Move slowly and be quiet and calm when you are around your pet, so they don't get frightened. If you are stroking your pet rabbit or rodent, be very gentle.

Rabbits should be held gently but firmly. Make sure the adult holding your rabbit uses one hand to support the back and bottom at all times and keeps all four feet held against them, as this will make your rabbit feel secure. Never, ever pick a rabbit up by the ears.

To pick up a guinea pig, put one hand around the shoulders and the other under the bottom. Never pick a hamster, rat, mouse or gerbil up by the tail. Use two hands to cup these types of rodent firmly but gently and support their bodies.

If you're handling hamsters, rats or mice, allow them to climb gently from one hand to another. Be careful not to hold them high up. Your pet could easily fall and be injured so handle them while you're sitting down.

Remember to move slowly and be quiet and calm around your pets to avoid frightening them. Always ask for an adult to help you handle your pet, and ideally ask the adult to pick the pet up.

Did you know?

Your pets may not like being picked up. They are more likely to enjoy spending time with you if you interact with them at ground level and offer them healthy treats.

Two's company

Some small pets love company. They get bored and lonely if they're kept on their own. Others are happier by themselves. Here's the low-down...

- Rabbits are very sociable and can suffer if they're on their own. Keep your pet with at least one other friendly rabbit. A good mix is a neutered male and a neutered female.

- Guinea pigs also like company. Keep two females together or a neutered male and one or more females.

- Mice live in big groups in the wild and can get very stressed if they're on their own. Keep an all-male or all-female group but make sure they're not fighting. Don't mix mice with other rodents – it spreads diseases and they may fight.

- Rats are also happiest in company. Young rats like to play with each other. Never keep a lone rat unless your vet tells you to.

- Some hamsters such as Syrian/Golden and Chinese hamsters fight if they're put in the same cage and can cause serious injuries. Dwarf species usually like living in groups, ideally with other hamsters that they have grown up with.

- Gerbils can be housed in groups of all-males or females – ideally they should have grown up together, to reduce the chance of fighting.

Did you know?

In the wild, gerbils live in large family groups. They use their sense of smell to work out who's who in their family.

Home, sweet home

Pet rabbits need a roomy enclosure to live in, with a shelter and a permanently attached exercise area.

Their main shelter can be a large hutch, converted shed or playhouse or an indoor pen, where they can rest, hide, and feel safe. Each rabbit should be able to stand upright on its back legs without its ears touching the roof and to stretch out fully when it's lying down.

Put the shelter somewhere quiet and calm, away from draughts and strong sunlight. If the shelter's outside, raise it off the ground so it doesn't get damp. Make sure it is safe and secure, so your rabbits can't escape and are protected from predators. Keep it dry and protected from the weather.

Rabbits also need a large, secure exercise area where they can run, jump, dig, graze on growing grass and play. They need to be able to access their exercise area at all times, so it should be permanently attached to the shelter. Make sure they have constant access to safe hiding places, in addition to the main shelter, where they can hide if they feel frightened or want to get away from their rabbit companions or people.

Rabbits like to have separate areas for eating, sleeping and going to the toilet. Line the bottom of the house with wood shavings or choose a house with a non-slip floor. A big pile of dust-free hay or straw in their 'bedroom area' makes a warm, cosy bed. Make sure that your rabbits have a place to go to the toilet. Line it with safe litter material like newspaper, shredded paper, hay or straw.

Top tip

Clean the toilet area daily and the whole house once a week. Add a little used bedding back afterwards, so the house smells familiar.

Did you know?

In winter, to make sure your rabbits are not too cold, you may need to move their enclosure indoors or into a shed or unused garage. Put in extra bedding to keep them warm. And don't forget – they'll still need space to exercise.

Bunny hops

Rabbits are full of energy and need plenty of exercise. Make sure they have a large, interesting space where they can run, jump and hop about, which is attached to their main shelter. This can be an outdoor run or even a bunny-proof room in your house.

The top three rabbit-friendly toys

1 Paper parcels: cut the handles from a paper bag, and add hay, shredded paper and some healthy treats inside for your bunnies to find. Or wrap their favourite food up in a parcel of brown paper.

2 Cardboard boxes and tubes: cut some holes in cardboard boxes to make fun hiding places, or stuff cardboard tubes with hay and healthy treats.

3 Bunny tunnels: you can buy rabbit tunnels that make brilliant toys. Or make your own tunnels from cardboard tubes or large, wide clay pipes.

Did you know?

For very happy bunnies, make your pets a digging box. You can:

- fill a large plant pot or litter tray with earth
- fill a cardboard box with shredded paper
- fill a sandpit with child-friendly sand

Rodent residences

Like rabbits, pet rodents need safe, secure places to live in. They also need plenty of space for exercising and playing. Here are some top housing hints and tips...

For guinea pigs...

- Your guinea pigs need a large house with enough room for each guinea pig to stand upright on their back legs and to stretch out fully when lying down. They also need a permanently attached exercise area to run around in. Make sure they have constant access to safe hiding places where they can hide if they feel frightened or want some space away from their guinea pig companions or people.
- Guinea pigs love exploring so put lots of pipes and tunnels in their run for them to play hide-and-seek.
- Safe wooden sticks make good toys for guinea pigs to gnaw. Don't give them anything made of plastic. It can harm them if they chew or swallow it.

For chinchillas...

- Chinchillas need a large wire mesh cage, with plenty of wood flooring areas provided so they don't damage their feet, and with plenty of space and platforms so they can jump safely.
- Keep their cage in a cool place, away from central heating and draughts.
- Chinchillas are shy animals. Make sure their home is in a quiet place and provide them with plenty of safe hiding places.
- Wood, rope, cardboard and pumice make suitable toys for chinchillas to chew. Don't give them anything made of plastic.
- Provide plenty of dust-free hay as bedding and a shallow container of chinchilla dust or fine sand so they can keep clean. Make sure this is changed regularly.

For hamsters...

- Keep your hamster(s) in a large cage with a snug, dark nest box for them to sleep in and use as a food store. Fill the nest box with suitable nesting material, such as hay or shredded paper. Never use fluffy material like cotton wool. Put the cage in a place where the lights go off at the same time each night (remember, hamsters are nocturnal). Keep the home away from the TV, computer or running water as the noise will disturb your pets.
- You might like to put a running wheel in the cage so your hamsters can use it to exercise. The wheel should be solid so your hamsters don't trap their feet and have a non-slip running surface.
- Add other toys, such as small boxes, empty toilet rolls and wooden chewing blocks for your hamsters to play with. These will also encourage your hamsters to move around while exploring their cage.

For gerbils...

- You can get a special house for gerbils, called a gerbilarium. It has solid glass walls and a wire-mesh top. It needs to be big enough for all of your gerbils to have space to dig, exercise and hide. Keep the home away from the TV, computer or running water as the noise will disturb your pets.
- Give your gerbils plenty of suitable bedding to dig and make tunnels in, as they would in the wild. A mixture of rough woodchips and hay are best for this.
- Gerbils also need nesting material to shred. You can use empty toilet rolls, egg boxes or cardboard boxes. Never use fluffy material, such as cotton wool.

For rats...

- Rats can be very active so they need a cage with plenty of space.
- Rats like dark places to hide and rest so provide plenty of shelters for them.
- Rats don't like high-pitched or sudden noises so put their cage somewhere quiet. Keep their home away from doorbells, alarms and telephones.
- Give your rats lots of hammocks and ropes to encourage them to climb and explore their home.

For mice...

- Mice can be very active so they need a cage with plenty of space. Keep the home away from the TV, computer or running water as the noise will disturb your pets.
- Mice like surfaces to scurry about and climb on, like shelves. Make sure they won't fall from them though.
- Give your mice lots of shredded paper, hay and tissues for making nests. They also need piles of deep bedding, such as shredded filter paper, to burrow into.
- Add other toys, such as small boxes, empty toilet rolls and wooden chewing blocks for your mice to play with.

Top tip

If you're going away, make sure you get someone to look after your pets. It's best if your pets can be looked after at home as rodents don't like to travel. If they have to go somewhere else, make sure they stay in their own cage, are kept in their social pair or group and give them something that smells familiar (like toys). Make sure that the person looking after them has clear instructions on how to care for your pets.

Dinner time!

Your pets need to eat a healthy diet. They also need constant access to fresh, clean water so they can have a drink day or night. Let's see what should be on the menu for rabbits or rodents.

Dos and don'ts for feeding all pets:

☑ **DO** check that your pets always have clean, fresh water, and make sure they don't freeze in winter.

☒ **DON'T** make any sudden changes to your pet's diet. It could make them ill.

WARNING: Always make sure food is suitable for your pet. If you are unsure, ask your vet for advice.

Did you know?

Rabbits, guinea pigs, chinchillas, rats and mice eat some of their own poo to help them get as much goodness as possible from their food.

Rabbits

☑ **DO** give your rabbits hay and access to growing grass to graze – grazing helps to prevent their teeth from growing too long.

☑ **DO** add a handful of safe, washed leafy green veg and herbs every day, as well as a small amount of special rabbit pellets. As an occasional treat, you can also give your pet a very small amount of carrot or fruit like a little piece of apple, but don't feed them too much as they are high in sugar.

☒ **DON'T** give your rabbits any grass clippings from the lawnmower. They'll upset their tummies and make them ill.

☒ **DON'T** feed your rabbit muesli-style foods, which are unhealthy.

Guinea pigs

☑ **DO** feed your guinea pig on hay, with some grass, guinea pig pellets and leafy greens.

☒ **DON'T** give your guinea pig citrus fruits like oranges or lemons.

Hamsters

☑ **DO** give your hamsters a balanced diet of special pelleted or mixed hamster food. You can also feed them small bits of suitable fruit and veg as part of their daily ration.

Rats

☑ **DO** give rats a balanced diet of special pelleted food, which contains all the nutritients they need.

☑ **DO** give rats an occasional small portion of fruit or vegetables or cooked egg as part of their daily food allowance, not extra.

☒ **DON'T** give your rats too much sweet and fatty food, such as seeds or cheese, which can make them overweight.

Gerbils

☑ **DO** buy special pellet or seed mixes for gerbils which give them all the goodness they need.

☑ **DO** add some suitable fruit, such as pear or apple, and some veggies, such as carrot or cucumber.

☑ **DO** check the gerbilarium regularly for hoarded food and remove any that is stale.

Mice

☑ **DO** give your mice a balanced diet – ask your vet for advice if you are not sure what to feed them.

☑ **DO** give them small amounts of fruit and vegetables as part of their daily diet, not as extra treats.

☒ **DON'T** give your mice lettuce, which can give them diarrhoea.

Chinchillas

☑ **DO** make sure your chinchilla always has plenty of hay available.

☑ **DO** give them a spoonful or two of chinchilla pellets every day.

☒ **DON'T** give them nuts and seeds, as they are too fatty.

☑ **DO** give root vegetables like carrots, leafy greens, dried fruit, or grains in very small amounts as a treat.

Did you know?

In the wild, rodents find their food by foraging about. Scatter some of their food around their cage so that your pet rodents can do the same.

The top four fur-care tips

Follow these top tips to keep your pets' fur in tip-top condition…

4 If your pets have got long hair, it can easily become dirty and matted. Brush your pets regularly. You can buy special grooming brushes, or use a baby's hairbrush or a soft toothbrush for tiny pets.

3 Chinchillas and gerbils need a dust bath for a short time every day to keep their fur clean. Fill a shallow tray with fine, clean sand or 'chinchilla dust'. Change it regularly to stop the sand getting dirty and remove it after use.

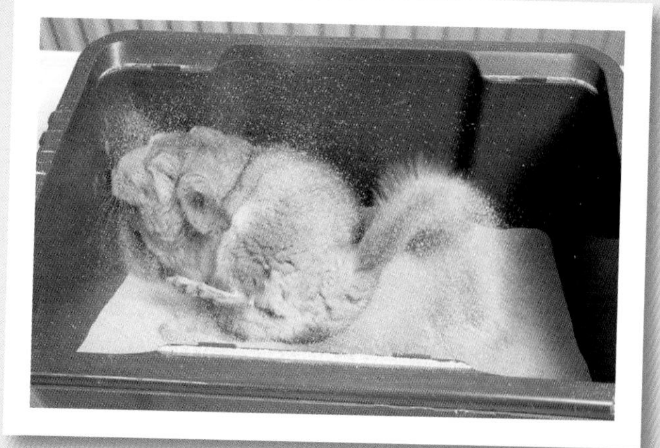

***Make sure your chinchilla can get in and out of the dust bath with ease.**

2 Mice sometimes pull out each other's whiskers or patches of fur. This may mean that they are getting stressed and may need more space. If they're fighting, ask a vet or other expert for advice.

1 Check your rats for bald patches. These may be caused by your rats grooming themselves too much or by a skin problem so it's best to check with a vet.

Did you know?

If your pet stops grooming itself, or starts pulling out its fur, or that of one of its companions, it might mean that it's ill or bored. It is best to take it to the vet's to check if anything is wrong.

Ask a vet

Part of being a good pet owner is making sure your pets are happy and healthy. Here are some frequently asked questions, answered by an RSPCA vet.

Q: How can I tell if my pets are feeling ill?

A: Check your pets every day for signs of illness, injury or changes in behaviour. Ask a responsible, knowledgeable person to do it if you're away. One sign that your pets may not be well is if his or her eating, drinking or toileting habits change or stop altogether. If you are at all worried about your pet, speak to your vet as soon as possible.

Q: Why does my pet need insurance?

A: Pet insurance is always a good idea. If your pet does fall ill, insurance can cover the cost of expensive treatment.

Q: Do I need to get my pets neutered?

A: Neutering's a simple operation that stops a pet having babies. If you want to keep male and female animals together, you should have them neutered so you don't suddenly find yourself with lots of extra pets to look after. It can also help to reduce the risk of fighting. Ask your vet for advice.

Q: Help! Why does my chinchilla keep losing clumps of its fur?

A: It might mean your chinchilla's feeling scared or stressed, or that he or she is ill. Take your chinchilla to the vet for a check-up and remember to be quiet and gentle around your pet.

Q: My pet's nails are getting too long. What shall I do?

A: Ask your vet or another pet-care specialist to trim them. Don't try to do it yourself – you might hurt your pet. Check your pet's nails every week and get them trimmed when necessary.

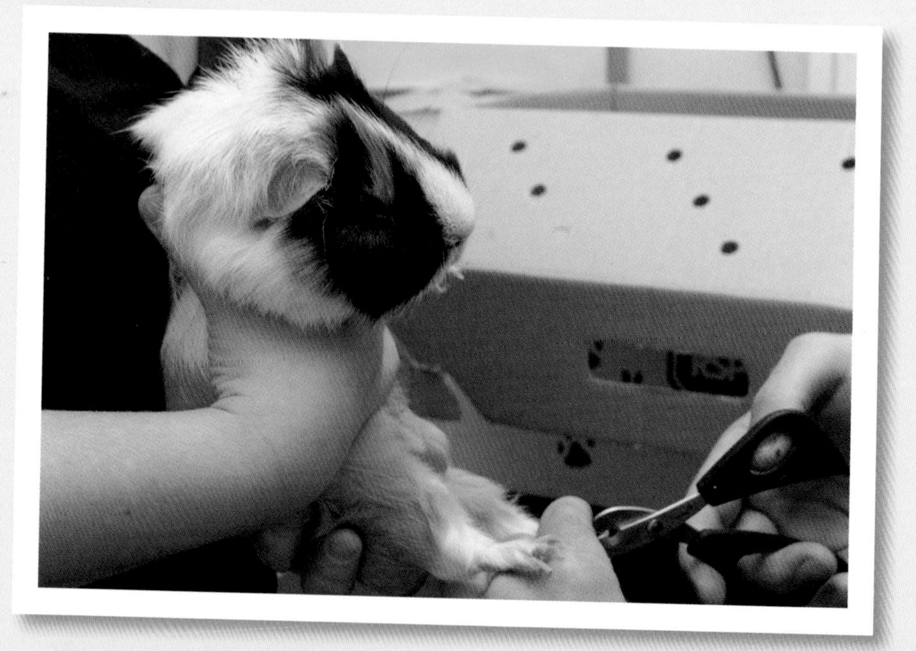

Q: Why do my gerbils thump their feet on the ground?

A: This is what gerbils do in the wild to warn each other of danger. Then the whole group can scamper into their burrows for safety.

Q: Why does my hamster gnaw at the bars of its cage?

A: It may be bored. Hamsters like to have things to do. Make sure it has a running wheel and lots of toys to play with. You can also arrange the inside of its cage so that it's more interesting for your pet.

Common problems in rabbits and rodents

Q: Does my pet need vaccinations?

A: Like dogs and cats, rabbits should be vaccinated. Your vet can advise you what will be needed and when.

Q: What should I do if I think my pet has worms?

A: Many pets can pick up worms from other animals, or from being in contact with them outside. Worms can make give pets a variety of health problems. Your vet can advise you on suitable worm treatments and how to prevent your pets from getting them.

Q. What is flystrike?

A: Flystrike happens when flies lay their eggs in the fur of animals and the maggots eat into their skin. It can make an animal very ill in a matter of hours. To prevent it, ensure that your pet is clean, particularly around their bottom. Clean toilet areas every day and ensure that bedding is changed frequently, especially in hot weather. If your pet lives outside, try to 'insect-proof' their enclosures. Check your pet regularly for injuries and sores and make sure these are treated by a vet immediately.

Keeping your pet safe

If your rabbits or guinea pigs live outside, you will need to take extra care to keep them safe.

☑ Make sure their enclosures are secure and that your pets are protected from predators such as foxes and that they have suitable places to hide, like tunnels, if they are feeling scared.

☑ Ensure their enclosure is protected from extremes of temperature, wind and rain.

☑ If temperatures drop low, make sure your rabbits or guinea pigs have plenty of clean, dry bedding. You may wish to add a cardboard box filled with hay to a corner of their enclosure, for added warmth.

☑ If you have cats or dogs, keep them away from your pet rabbits or rodents. Never leave them together unsupervised.

Rabbits and rodents quiz

1. What does 'lagomorph' mean?

a) pear-shaped b) hare-like
c) star-shaped

2. What are white rabbits a sign of?

a) good luck b) bad luck c) good weather

3. Rabbits can do the following:

a) hop and jump b) dig c) stand upright on their back legs

4. How big is a capybara?

a) the size of a sheep b) the size of a guinea pig
c) the size of an elephant

5. Rats can an occasional treat of...

a) a little cooked egg b) cheese c) seeds

6. Which rodents purr?

a) gerbils **b)** hamsters **c)** guinea pigs

7. Where do gerbils live in the wild?

a) on mountains **b)** near rivers **c)** in deserts

8. Which pets like living in pairs or groups?

a) mice **b)** guinea pigs **c)** rabbits

9. What are baby rabbits called?

a) pinkies **b)** kittens **c)** cubs

10. In Aztec legend, which animal lives on the moon?

a) a rat **b)** a lion **c)** a rabbit

Answers

1. b), **2.** a), **3.** all three, **4.** a), **5.** a), **6.** c), **7.** c), **8.** all of them! **9.** b), **10.** c)

Rabbit and rodents trivia

Did you know some of these amazing facts about rabbits and rodents?

- When a rabbit is frightened or injured, they can scream loudly to alert other rabbits to danger.

- In the wild, a rabbit warren of interconnecting burrows can cover an area the size of 30 tennis courts!

- Some species of wild gerbil can leap a distance of more than 3.5 metres.

- Some wild hamsters create tunnels up to 2 metres below the soil surface in winter, for warmth.

- Guinea pigs are also known as cavies.

- In the wild, gerbils can store up to 60 kilograms of food in their burrows.

- A male guinea pig is called a boar. A female is a sow.

- A group of rats is known as a pack or a mischief.

- Chinchillas in the Andes mountains can live at more than 4,000 metres above sea level.

- In the wild, chinchillas live in colonies of more than 100 animals.

All about the RSPCA

The RSPCA, or Royal Society for the Prevention of Cruelty to Animals, was founded in 1824 in London. It was the first British animal welfare charity and was originally mostly concerned with the welfare of animals such as pit ponies that worked down the coal mines. The charity also worked with the hundreds of thousands of animals that served in the military during the First and Second World Wars.

Since then, the RSPCA has worked tirelessly to improve the lives of millions of animals, including those kept as pets and farm animals. It has 170 branches around the country, where staff and volunteers care for the animals that come into the centres. Many are re-homed after they have been nursed back to health and enjoy happiness with their new owners.

By educating people about animal welfare, the RSPCA aims to make sure that all animals live healthy, happy lives and are treated with compassion and respect.

For further expert advice on caring for the pets featured in this book go to: **www.rspca.org.uk**.

RSPCA

Index

Also available

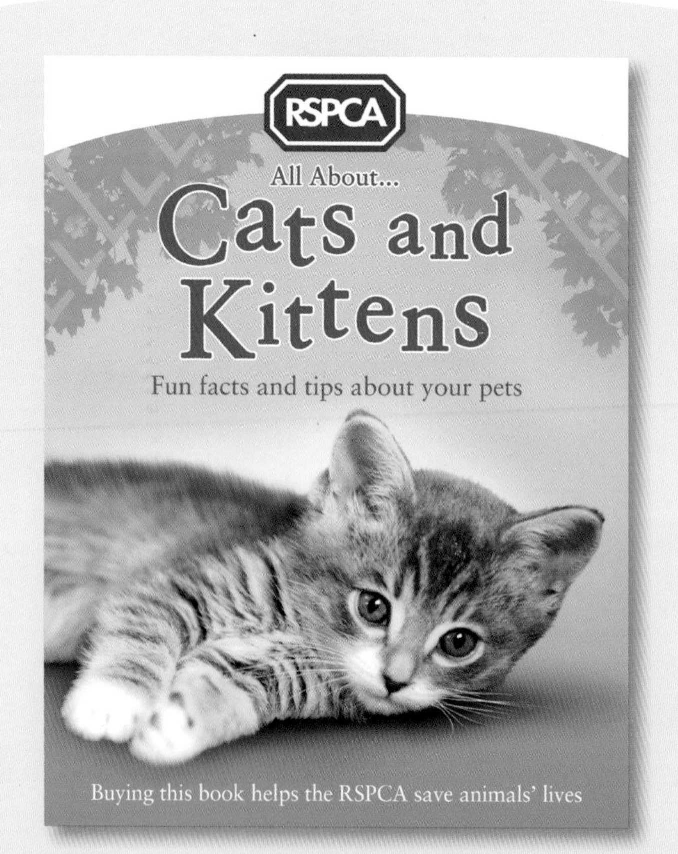

Picture credits. Front cover: Falk Herrmann/Gettyimages, ©Aflo Relax/Masterfile ; page 6: Becky Murray/RSPCA Photolibrary; page 7: Chris Brignell/RSPCA Photolibrary; page 8, left: © Minden Pictures/Masterfile, middle: © Robert Harding Images/Masterfile, right: © Minden Pictures/Masterfile; page 9: Angela Hampton/RSPCA Photolibrary; pages 10, 11, and 12, top: © Minden Pictures/Masterfile; page 12, bottom: Mint Images - Art Wolfe/GettyImages; page 13, top: © Minden Pictures/Masterfile, bottom: Joel Sartore/GettyImages; page 14-15: © Masterfile; page 15: © Martin Ruegner/Masterfile; page 17: © Masterfile; page 18: Becky Murray/RSPCA Photolibrary; page 19: © sushkonastya/Masterfile; page 20: © pressmaster/Masterfile; page 21: © Aflo Reflex/Masterfile; page 23: © Masterfile; page 24: Angela Hampton/RSPCA Photolibrary; page 25: Angela Hampton/RSPCA Photolibrary; page 26: Chris Brignell/RSPCA Photolibrary; page 27: Becky Murray/RSPCA Photolibrary; page 28: Chris Brignell/RSPCA Photolibrary; page 29: © isselee/Masterfile; page 30: © Minden Pictures/Masterfile; page 31: © gsagi/Masterfile; page 32, top: © Minden Pictures/Masterfile, middle: © Robert Harding Images/Masterfile, bottom: © Minden Pictures/Masterfile; page 33, top: © Holger Ehlers/Masterfile, second: © Robert Harding Images/Masterfile, third: © Minden Pictures/Masterfile, bottom: David Chapman/ RSPCA Photolibrary; page 34: © blewis/Masterfile, bottom: ©Gerhard Schulz/GettyImages; page 35, top: Stephen Dalton/GettyImages, bottom: © Minden Pictures/Masterfile, bottom left & right: © Minden Pictures/Masterfile; page 36: © Masterfile; page 37: © bluerain22/Masterfile; page 39, left: © Masterfile, right: © Pakhnyushchyy/Masterfile; page 40: Isselee/Masterfile; page 41: © foodanddrinkphotos/Masterfile; page 42: © ClassicStock/Masterfile; page 43, top: © ClassicStock/Masterfile, bottom: © imagebroker/Masterfile; page 44 & 45, top: E A Janes/RSPCA Photolibrary, bottom: © Cusp and Flirt/Masterfile; page 46, top: Angela Hampton/RSPCA Photolibrary, bottom: Chris Brignell/RSPCA Photolibrary; page 47, top: © Minden Pictures/Masterfile, bottom: Chris Brignell/RSPCA Photolibrary; page 48: E A Janes/RSPCA Photolibrary; pages 49, 50, 51: Chris Brignell/ RSPCA Photolibrary; page 52: Philip Toscano/ RSPCA Photolibrary; page 54-55: Becky Murray/RSPCA Photolibrary; page 55: Philip Toscano/ RSPCA Photolibrary; page 56, & 57, top: Chris Brignell/RSPCA Photolibrary; bottom: © isselee/Masterfile; page 58, top: © Masterfile, bottom & 59: © isselee/Masterfile; page 60: Philip Toscano/ RSPCA Photolibrary; page 62 & 64: Angela Hampton/RSPCA Photolibrary; page 65: © isselee/Masterfile; page 66: Philip Toscano/ RSPCA Photolibrary; page 68: © Dorling Kindersley; page 69: Philip Toscano/ RSPCA Photolibrary; page 70: E A Janes/RSPCA Photolibrary; page 71: Angela Hampton/RSPCA Photolibrary; page 72: Andrew Forsyth/RSPCA Photolibrary; page 73: Joe Murphy/RSPCA Photolibrary; page 74: © isselee/Masterfile; page 75: © Masterfile; page 77 top: © Masterfile, middle: E A Janes/RSPCA Photolibrary, bottom: © Cusp and Flirt/Masterfile; page 78, top: Chris Brignell/RSPCA Photolibrary, middle: E A Janes/RSPCA Photolibrary, bottom: © Ragnar/Masterfile; page 79, top & bottom: © Minden Pictures/Masterfile; page 80: Philip Toscano/ RSPCA Photolibrary; page 81: Angela Hampton/RSPCA Photolibrary; page 82, top: Joe Murphy/RSPCA Photolibrary, bottom: Angela Hampton/RSPCA Photolibrary; page 83: Chris Brignell/RSPCA Photolibrary; page 84: Andrew Forsyth/RSPCA Photolibrary; page 85: © trgowanlock/Masterfile; page 87: Andrew Forsyth/RSPCA Photolibrary; page 88, top: © Minden Pictures/Masterfile, second: Becky Murray/RSPCA Photolibrary, third: © Martin Ruegner/Masterfile, bottom: Chris Brignell/ RSPCA Photolibrary; page 89, top & second: E A Janes/RSPCA Photolibrary, third: © Ragnar/Masterfile, fourth: Angela Hampton/RSPCA Photolibrary, bottom: © sushkonastya/ Masterfile; page 90: Dorling Kindersley; page 91, top: RSPCA Photolibrary, bottom: RSPCA Photolibrary; page 93: Joe Murphy/RSPCA Photolibrary